A Raccoon's First Year

by Dorcas MacClintock
Photographs by Ellan Young

CHARLES SCRIBNER'S SONS NEW YORK

ACKNOWLEDGMENTS

A special thanks to Pat Canning for her work with orphan
raccoons and for her help, which made this book possible.
Thanks to Dorcas MacClintock,
whose home is a raccoon's and a photographer's paradise.
For good advice and more raccoon help I would like to thank
Kaye Anderson, Jean Craighead George, Tana Hoban and
Alan, Roz and Paul Wood, as well as my own three naturalists—
Melissa, Sarah, and Andy Young.
E.Y.

I am grateful to Lee Deadrick,
whose regard for raccoons led to the collaboration
of photographer and author.
D.M.

Library of Congress Cataloging in Publication Data
MacClintock, Dorcas.   A raccoon's first year.
Summary: Describes how the author raised an
orphaned raccoon cub so that it could eventually
resume its life in the wild.
1. Raccoons—Juvenile literature.   2. Raccoons
as pets—Juvenile literature.   [1. Raccoons.
2. Wild animals as pets]   I. Young, Ellan, ill.   II. Title.
QL737.C26M33   639'.974443   82-788
ISBN 0-684-17421-9   AACR2

3 5 7 9 11 13 15 17 19   Q/C   20 18 16 14 12 10 8 6 4 2

Printed in the United States of America

FOR MELISSA

E.Y.

Wild animal babies found in late spring or early summer usually have not been abandoned. Wild mothers often leave their young to go off in search of food. The babies should be left alone.

This week-old raccoon cub, found beneath a sycamore tree, is an orphan. Too young to have tumbled from a nursery den, she may have been dropped when a mother raccoon was forced to move her cubs from one den tree to another. Placed with a flannel blanket for snuggling in an open-top box, the tiny cub was left until late that night at the base of the big tree. But the female raccoon did not return.

The cub's small body curls comfortably in the cupped hands of her human parent. The cub's head, too heavy to hold up, is large for her body. Soft *vibrissae*, or whiskers, grow from both sides of her muzzle. Her eyes, sealed shut, are surrounded by two halves of the dark facial mask that is a raccoon characteristic. Soft white-furred ear flaps fall forward over still-sealed ear openings.

When the cub is carried in a hat, her tiny forepaws or hands,

5

with palms and fingers that are dark-skinned and soft, work back and forth to feel the brim. Touch is the most highly developed of the raccoon's five senses. Even the long hairs that project beyond the cub's down-curved claws increase her sense of touch.

For the first three weeks of life, except when they are suckling, raccoon cubs huddle for shared warmth in a furry heap at the bottom of their tree-cavity nursery. Hungry and untended, the cub squirms and cries. In the dry tree-hollow den she and her three siblings had been cared for by the mother raccoon. By roughly licking each cub's round tummy and small rump to stimulate urination and defecation, the female cleaned her babies and kept the nursery den free of any odor that might have attracted a predator.

To simulate the mother raccoon's cleaning, the cub's human parent uses a piece of warm, damp cotton to rub and clean her underside. More comfortable now, the cub's crying gives way to low churrs of content.

The cub's small, blunt muzzle is adapted for suckling. She soon learns to feed from a pet nurser filled with warm-to-the-touch *Esbilac*, a formula made especially for baby mammals.

Settled in her den box with the warm flannel blanket and a soft plush bear as a substitute littermate, the cub goes to sleep. Then it is time to call the state department of environmental protection to obtain a permit for keeping the cub until she is old enough to live on her own in the wild.

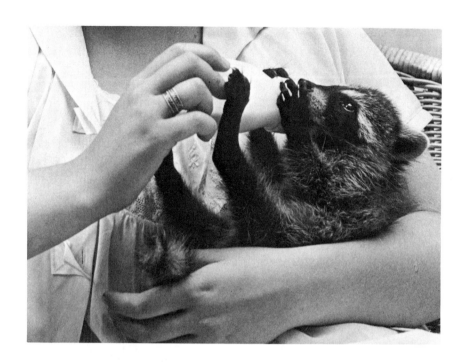

8

A baby's bottle with a soft *preemie* nipple has replaced the pet nurser.

When she is three weeks old, the cub's eyes open. It is a slow process, signalled by a tiny opening at the inner corner of one eyeslit. By the time this first eye is open, the other is half open. For a week or so the cub's eyes have a misty appearance and her vision is blurred. When she crawls about outside the den box she blunders into chair legs and other objects in her path. Now, at five weeks, the cub has no difficulty focusing on her bottle.

The cub's dark mask and nose-to-forehead streak are well defined. Including the dark tip, her tail has six rings. Eager to explore, she almost *never* holds still. Sometimes she is rowdy and so she is named Ruffian.

Ruffian's forepaws are like small human hands, each with two shorter outside fingers and three longer middle ones. The soft-skinned underside of her fingers and palms are supplied with many tiny tubelike sensory receptors, each one containing a nerve-fiber ending.

Feeling and probing become a way of life for the cub. So keen is her sense of touch that often she can feel and manipulate a treasure pulled from a pocket while her eyes are riveted straight ahead.

9

In rough-and-tumble play, ankles become biting targets. Ruffian likes nothing better than to be swung aloft. Her claws are useful for clinging, even when she is upside down.

Play is an important part of a raccoon cub's development. Stalking, pouncing, wrestling, and chasing, which Ruffian enjoys with cat or dog or person instead of with siblings, perfect actions she will use later in capturing prey and protecting herself.

Like a small child, Ruffian plays until she is exhausted. Then it is time for a nap. Times to sleep are interspersed with playtime and feeding time. A real bed is comfortable. And so is the top of the laundry hamper. A forepaw over the face keeps out the light.

11

On a first venture outdoors, eleven-week-old Ruffian tags close to her human parent's heels. She churrs, a constant low grumbling call that is used to maintain contact between cub and mother raccoon and among littermates. Curious about everything, she pauses to feel for a cricket in the grass. Finding herself left behind, she calls *whoo?*, then bounds to catch up.

Soon Ruffian is more confident and goes off on her own.

12

While exploring at the base of a tree, she meets a cat. And, since she is not sure about the cat, she climbs. For raccoons, there is safety in tree climbing. Small but strong forelimbs haul the cub's pear-shaped body up the trunk, while her hindfeet, one and then the other, assist in the climb.

Of course, cats can climb, too. But cats are seldom the raccoon's enemy. Such nighttime hunters as owls and bobcats menace young raccoons. But it is man with his dogs, guns, traps, and automobiles who is the raccoon's major predator.

14

A ladder invites climbing. And the barn loft, filled with sweet-smelling bales of hay, is an interesting place to explore.

Ruffian bounds along a fence rail, practicing *arboreal*, or tree-climbing, techniques. She slows to walk over a post. Her rolling stride appears to anticipate loss of balance.

She clings, belly close to the rail. A nudge from the horse upsets her. Ruffian catches herself. Upside down and hanging on, she moves hand over hand to the next post where she regains her right-side-up position.

15

Tree bark, at least the rough bark of some kinds of trees, is made for raccoons to climb. Ruffian's stout, curved, sharp claws make it easy for her to reach this favorite tree fork, a place where she feels secure.

Sometimes curiosity takes a young raccoon out on a limb. Striding along a branching tree trail, Ruffian feels the long, thin branch sag beneath her weight. She molds her small body to the branch and clings desperately. After much scrambling, flailing of hindlimbs, and frantic clutching with her forearms, she manages to turn herself around and return to the tree's trunk.

The cub is frightened by this experience and churrs for help. Her confidence for headfirst descent, or even for backing down the trunk, is gone. When she feels a hand grasp the fur over her shoulders, she loosens her bark clawhold and is carried indoors for a nap.

Another day brings another adventure. At first fearful of water, Ruffian churrs anxiously from the edge of the pool. She wets her forepaws, then thrusts her nose in and splutters. In no time she discovers the nature of water and delights in underwater churning.

With hindfeet firmly planted on the pool's rock edge, the cub dabbles, unafraid of the deep water. She moves her forepaws faster and faster as the water splashes and swirls. When her body fur gets wet, she gives a vigorous head-to-tail shake and *almost* falls into the pool.

There are other places to find water. And perhaps even to meet another raccoon. *Whoo-oo?* queries Ruffian. The other cub makes no reply.

19

A young raccoon must be wary. In the outdoor world any strange sound, sight, or smell causes Ruffian to press close to her human parent. When exploring indoors, Ruffian is more confident. A desk, with pencil pot, a philodendron plant, and books to finger, occupies her for some minutes.

The trespasser is caught and scurries off into the kitchen. She finds that she cannot squeeze behind the stove and, in desperation, heads into an overturned pitcher.

After a reprimand, Ruffian finds reassurance in suckling on her bottle. But suckling soon gives way to pulling and snapping the rubber nipple with her sharp incisor teeth. A mother raccoon would never stand for such behavior.

In the wild, a cub Ruffian's age is too old for nursing. At three months the weaning process is underway and cubs forage at night with their mother. And, by this stage, the family has moved from tree nursery den to a ground den in a hollow log, or beneath the roots of a blown-down tree, or on a tussock of marsh grass.

23

24   For raccoons, ears are targets for biting. Perhaps this is one reason their own ears are conspicuously marked, white and black. Sometimes in play Ruffian nips a human ear.

The three-and-a-half-month-old cub has lost most of her needlelike *deciduous*, or milk teeth. Her permanent incisors, six upper and six lower, are sharp biting teeth. Her four canine teeth and some of her premolars also have been replaced, and a first molar tooth is breaking through the gum.

It is time to prepare the cub for a life on her own. Ruffian is fed outside now. A bird feeder in the cherry tree makes an ideal feeding platform. Chunky, dry dog food, fruits, Fig Newtons, and all kinds of food scraps are among the finger foods she carefully chews and swallows. Climbing out on a limb, she discovers cherries. To reach the ripest, reddest treats she sometimes relies on just her hindfeet for support and uses her tail for balance. She chews each cherry with upturned head, so that the sweet juice trickles down her throat.

In the wild, raccoons raid the nests of ducks and other ground-nesting birds. When Ruffian is given an egg she grasps it between her forepaws. Then she puts it down and rolls it beneath her palms. Finally she picks it up again and, turning her head to one side, bites through the shell. Yolk and white spill out. Ruffian laps with enthusiasm, careful to keep her long white vibrissae drawn back against her face.

In the grass Ruffian finds crickets, grasshoppers, and beetles to pounce on. The captured insect is pressed between palms and fingers and rolled back and forth. Then it is eaten.

Toward the end of summer, Ruffian finds acorns. Foraging for them is less exciting than hunting for live prey. Near the base of an oak tree, the cub sits back to crush open an acorn she has rolled between her forepaws. In the wild, acorns form most of a raccoon's fall diet. Their carbohydrate content is important for fall fattening.

27

When she is indoors now, Ruffian lives up to her name. Here she leaves the scene of a crime.

In no time she is into more mischief. Dabbling in a goldfish tank, she rakes her fingers through the gravel and *almost* grasps the frightened fish.

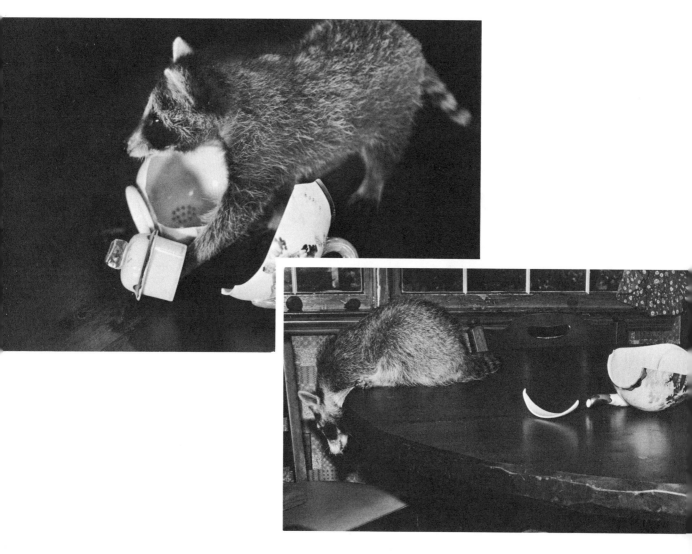

30

Ruffian's den for the day is a box in the closet.

After a long sleep, she leaves the house through a hole in the screen door. Her hindfeet turn backward, like a squirrel's, to slow her descent.

In the driveway Ruffian finds a car. Tires have interesting smells and treads are good for climbing. A raccoon always feels secure with its body pressed into a small space, such as this one between tire and fender. When she is on her own the cub will learn to fear cars and to avoid roads.

Dogs are also to be reckoned with. Some are friendly, especially with a cub they know. Others are too rough, even for Ruffian. But a dog cannot climb. A young raccoon usually takes refuge in a tree. But a wily older raccoon sometimes matches wits with a dog and leads it on a long chase before finally treeing or going into water to throw its pursuer off the scent.

32

34

While exploring near the edge of the woods, Ruffian pauses. She sits up on her haunches and turns in the direction of a rustling sound. Intently, she watches and listens. Then, satisfied there is nothing to fear, she shuffles into the woods.

Berries and fruits can be had by climbing and reaching. Ruffian, raised by a human parent, forages in the daytime. But raccoons, for the most part, are nocturnal.

The raccoon's round eye is adapted for nighttime vision. A

large and cone-shaped cornea (the circular, transparent covering of the lens) and a large pupillary opening let in the maximum amount of night light. Just behind the light-sensitive retina is a layer of flat, tile-like cells, the *tapetum*. The tapetum reflects light back through the retina to increase the stimulation of its rod-shaped visual cells.

The tapetum also causes a raccoon's eyes to shine orange-red in the beam of a flashlight.

Ruffian returns in late afternoon. Probably she does not want to miss feeding time.

She still churrs contentedly when she is picked up and held.

Raccoons have two patterns of feeding that vary with time of year and availability of foods: *dry feeding* (when scouting for berries, insects, mice, acorns, and nuts in summer and fall) and wet feeding or *dabbling* (when searching for aquatic prey along stream and lake margins in spring and summer).

Raccoons like to dabble. Wetting, it appears, increases their ability to feel. This may be why a captive raccoon sometimes douses its food. Not to *wash* the food, as often is said, but just to enjoy the sensation of make-believe dabbling.

Ruffian dabbles along a stream bank. Her forepaws touch the water. At first her splayed fingers make idling movements. Then she feels the sandy bottom and begins to work her forepaws with a rotary motion. Her shoulders revolve as forepaws slither over sand and fingers probe and turn over pebbles. Now and again she looks down. In shallow pools her dabbling is slow and methodical. She probes under rocks and searches the bottom. Her long, soft-skinned fingers are sensitive to the feel of anything alive, mussels, tadpoles, crayfish, or minnows.

A crayfish is felt. Ruffian lunges. Her tail jerks upward as she seizes her prey. Grasping the invertebrate just behind its claws, first in her forepaws and then in her teeth, she carries it to a nearby bouldertop. There she holds down the flailing pincers with her forepaws and bites into the flipping tail. She settles back on her haunches to chew the white meat from the hard outer shell, discarding head and pincers. Nothing tastes better than a crayfish.

Attracted by minnows, their sides flashing silver, Ruffian wades in. She pursues the fish upstream where water flows swiftly between boulders. Her dabbling becomes frenzied. She catches one minnow, biting off its head and then consuming the rest, and then another minnow.

Although Ruffian would rather just wade, dabbling sometimes takes her in over her elbows to swim across a deep stream pool. She is a good swimmer then, paddling with head up and tail straight out, her body only half submerged.

39

Her vibrissae, usually folded back against her face, are brought forward to form a circlet around her muzzle. Without these stiff sensory hairs to maintain contact with the water surface, a raccoon would have difficulty keeping its nose above water.

40

As autumn approaches, daylight hours shorten. Like other wild animals, Ruffian is preparing for winter. Black-tipped guard hairs grow longer and give a lustrous sheen to her coat. The brownish underfur that will insulate her body, preventing excessive loss of heat, grows denser.

She also gains weight, though not as much as an adult raccoon does during the fall. Fall fattening, the raccoon's way of readying for a time of cold, snow, and food scarcity, is common among *carnivores* (mammals of the order Carnivora, which includes dogs, bears, weasels, cats, and raccoons) that are *omnivores*. Raccoons, like bears, eat both plant and animal foods. They take advantage of an abundance of acorns, nuts, and other fall foods and fatten on them. Although most of Ruffian's first-year food intake is utilized for growth rather than for fattening, by late fall her small rump will be padded by a blanket of fat just beneath the skin. This time of fall fattening causes raccoons to forage widely and search out all food supplies. Ruffian responds to the urge even indoors, by working through the kitchen-wastebasket contents.

A growing sluggishness is apparent. Ruffian sleeps more now. Almost any napping place will do. A high shelf in the garage is one place she is apt to be found.

During waking hours Ruffian spends more time on her own. As they near adult size, young raccoons have an inherent urge to wander. Fall is dispersal time for some cubs. For others the urge to disperse, or leave home, is suppressed by the coming of winter cold and snow. Their first winter is spent in the shared warmth of a family den. Then, as yearlings in the following spring, they wander off to find living places of their own.

Perhaps in search of a winter den, Ruffian stops to explore a hollow log. This tree trunk, toppled by wind, no longer shelters a raccoon.

Protection from wind, rain, and snow is an important factor in selecting a winter den. An ideal den is situated about 8 meters (just over 26 feet) up in a large tree. The south-facing entrance is just large enough for a raccoon to squeeze in and out.

Dens are formed when lightning, wind, or fire injures a tree trunk, or when a large limb breaks off to form a slash opening that is enlarged in time by weathering and decay. Sometimes a cavity, started by the hammerings of a woodpecker and enlarged by decay, gnawing insects, and small mammal inhabitants, becomes suitable for raccoon use.

43

Ruffian found a winter denning place and did not return from her woodland venture. Weeks later she is glimpsed high up in the winter-bare branches of a tree.

Almost every night she visits the feeder in the cherry tree where she knows food has been put out for her. It is cold now and raccoon appetites are reduced. Ruffian spends less and less time foraging at night. And on blustery cold nights, or when it snows, she stays snug in her tree den.

Raccoons winter den to sleep away times of bitter cold and deep snow, often for days and even for weeks at a stretch. A winter-denned raccoon, with head and forepaws rolled beneath its chest, hindfeet pulled up into its body fur, and nose near its tail, is protected from cold by its well-furred, fat-padded back and rump. And its stored body fat provides winter sustenance, enough to maintain near-normal body temperature and an only slightly slowed rate of metabolism or bodily function.

By late winter, accustomed to cold and snow and hungry again as her fat reserve diminishes, Ruffian again comes nightly to the feeder in the cherry tree. Another raccoon, a large male, comes with her. It is mating time. For several days, before moving on, he shares Ruffian's tree den.

On a sunny day in May, a raccoon is spotted, high up in a tall maple. Seconds later, a small masked face peers cautiously from behind the sleeping form of its mother. The den is a nursery.

46

The mother raccoon—it *is* Ruffian—dozes on her back. Her left forearm is draped protectively over the den sill to prevent her two curious cubs from climbing up and tumbling out.

Don't you agree that the small cub sniffing the air outside the den is a replica of Ruffian?

Index